OVERCOMING ADDICTION WITH 5 ENERGETIC PRINCIPLES

Transforming Destructive Energy To
Get Real and Get Sober

COURSE SCRIPT / INDIVIDUAL SESSION SCRIPT

Jeffrey Cohen

Copyright © 2013 Sober Jeffrey Creations

All rights reserved.

ISBN:1490914870
ISBN-13:9781490914879

DEDICATION

This book is dedicated to all the people who have helped me along my journey to freedom from self-destruction. This includes every person to ever walk into my life—because each of you has helped me to overcome addiction. For those of you who struggle, do not quit before the miracle. It took me 18 years to get sobriety!

I lived a reclusive life, mistaking isolation as being emancipated, free. Free from the demands of people. By not being accountable I lived the belief that people were a burden. The burden would suck me dry. My needs would never be met. So I resigned myself to this life until one day I realized that my seclusion from the world was a prison for my soul. A death of the worst kind.

Mired in sex, love, meth, nicotine, and alcohol addiction for my entire life, let this book serve as proof that one can emerge to find god and his rightful place of being alive in this world. I dedicate this book to those who never made it out of the shame cycle.

My recovery model is about transforming destructive energy into getting real and getting sober. I used 5 Energetic Principles to make this happen. It is a pleasure to share this with all of you. God Bless!

Jeffrey Cohen

CONTENTS

THE VISION	8
THE AGENDA	9
RULES	11
FRIDAY AUGUST 23	11
CHECK IN AND PARTICIPANT INTRODUCTIONS	11
JEFFREY COHEN PERSONAL STORY AND OVERCOMING ADDICTION	13
FACING THE TRUTH PATTERNS OF ADDICTION	26
WITHDRAWAL EXPERIENTIAL	29
WITHDRAWAL INTEGRATION	30
PROCESS GROUP NIGHT 1	30
SATURDAY AUGUST 24	31
YOGA NIDRE	31

AVOIDING TOXIC PEOPLE, PLACES, AND THINGS	31
FACING FEELINGS	32
PROCESS GROUP FACING FEELINGS	34
GROUP STORY TELLING	34
SUNDAY AUGUST 25	35
FEEL GOOD YOGA	35
HEALTHY REPLACEMENTS FOR THE ADDICTION	35
NEW LIFE ENERGY PROCESS GROUP	36
GENERAL PROCESS GROUP	36
MOVIE NIGHT	36
MONDAY AUGUST 26	36
SPIRITUAL SERVICE	36
FINAL PROCESS GROUP	37
FAREWELL AND CLOSING REMARKS	37
SUPPLIES	38
INDIVIDUAL SESSION SCRIPT	39

SESSION 1: DENIAL ENERGY	**39**
SESSION 2: WITHDRAWAL ENERGY	**41**
SESSION 3: TOXIC OUTSIDE ENERGY	**46**
SESSION 4: FEELINGS ENERGY	**49**
SESSION 5: NEW LIFE ENERGY	**58**
SESSION 6: SUMMARY	**60**

THE VISION

OVERCOMING ADDICTION
INTENSIVE 4 DAY UPSCALE RETREAT
CENTER CITY PHILADELPHIA HOTEL (TBD)

Friday, Aug 23rd starting @ 9AM thru Mon. Aug. 26th ending 3PM

- ☑ FOR BUSY PROFESSIONALS
- ☑ TARGETED TO ADDICTS
- ☑ TAUGHT BY RECOVERY EXPERT
- ☑ ANONYMOUS
- ☑ JUMP START YOUR RECOVERY

-Simple, Practical Tools, And Intensive Work In Small Group to Challenge You To Recover **USING NEW ADDICTION RECOVERY MODEL**

- **Transforming destructive energy into getting real and getting sober.** Using 5 Energetic Principles to make this happen.

-Open To ANY ADDICT: Substances, Food, Nicotine, Sex, Love, Porn, Gambling, etc.

-Private Rooms, Blocked Television, Must stay on site at the hotel the entire time

-Challenging, Rewarding, Advanced ENERGY WORK

-COSTS $2,200 per person which includes private room, meals, Intensive CORE teaching, materials, space rental and entertainment for the entire 4 days
-YOU MUST CALL JEFFREY COHEN to discuss advanced sign up
-CALL 215-687-4451; PHILLYRECOVERYEXPERT@GMAIL.COM
-WEBSITE http://joeyelvira21.wix.com/addictionphilly

-NO INSURANCE ACCEPTED
-PAYMENT BY PAYPAL OR CHECK
-Must show up sober on that Friday to attend the event. We will discuss over the phone

THE AGENDA

FRIDAY AUGUST 23

9AM – 9:45AM	Check In, Opening, and Participant Introductions
9:45AM-10:30	J. Cohen Story, Presentation of the Overcoming Addiction Model
10:30AM-10:45	Break
10:45AM-12:30	Facing The Truth – Patterns of Addiction
12:30PM-1:30PM	Lunch
1:30PM-2:00PM	Quiet Time
2:00PM-3:30PM	Withdrawal Experiential
3:30PM-3:45PM	Break
3:45PM-5:00PM	Withdrawal Integration
5:00PM-6:00PM	Use The Facilities, Read, Relax
6:00PM-8:00PM	Dinner
8:00PM-10:00PM	Process Group
10:00PM	Retire for the night. Go to individual rooms.

SATURDAY AUGUST 24

7AM – 7:30AM	Guided Morning Meditation-Yoga -Nidre
7:30AM-8:30AM	Breakfast
8:30AM-9:00AM	Quiet Time
9AM-11AM	Avoiding Toxic People, Places, Things
11AM-11:15	Break
11:15AM-12:45	Facing Feelings
12:45PM-1:45	Lunch
1:45PM-3:00	Use the Facilities, Read, Relax
3:00PM-5:00PM	Process Group Facing Feelings
5:00PM-6:00PM	Quiet Time
6:00PM-8:00PM	Dinner
8:00PM-10:00PM	GROUP STORY TELLING
10:00PM	Retire for the night. Go to individual rooms.

SUNDAY AUGUST 25

7AM – 7:30AM	Gentle Exercise and Movement –Feel Good Yoga
7:30AM-8:30AM	Breakfast
8:30AM-9:00AM	Quiet Time
9AM-11AM	Healthy Replacements For The Addiction
11AM-11:15	Break
11:15AM-12:45	New Life Energy – Process Group
12:45PM-1:45	Lunch
1:45PM-3:00	Use the Facilities, Read, Relax
3:00PM-5:00PM	General Process Group
5:00PM-6:00PM	Social Hour – Healthy Snacks & Beverages
500PM-6:00PM	Quiet Time
6:00PM-8:00PM	Dinner
8:00PM-10:00PM	MOVIE NIGHT
10:00PM	Retire for the night. Go to individual rooms.

MONDAY AUGUST 26

7AM – 8AM	Spiritual Service – "Heal Thyself"
8:00AM-9:00AM	Breakfast
9:00AM-10:00AM	Vacate Rooms - Quiet Time
10:00-12:00	FINAL PROCESS GROUP
12:00-1:00PM	Lunch
1:00PM-3:00PM	Farewell, Closing Remarks

RULES

No cell phones.
No contact with outside world.
No television.
Listen to the radio if you need to.
No masturbation. No substance use of any kind.
No smoking cigarettes
Everyone's voice matters

FRIDAY AUGUST 23

CHECK IN AND PARTICIPANT INTRODUCTIONS

-Welcome to Overcoming Addiction Intensive
-Life Changing Experience For Everyone
-I'm Jeffrey Cohen and I have developed a model for overcoming Addiction based on 5 Energetic Principles that I've used in my own 18 year struggle to recover from addiction. It is a model based on CORE Energetics, and I'm a Certified Core Energetics Practitioner.
-This is not the only way
-Goal of this intensive is to give you an experiential of overcoming addiction and empower you with transformative tools to overcome addiction.
-Safe space, beautiful hotel and room. The bathrooms are in the hall. Use them if you need to and just come back!
-Try to be open
-Everything we talk about is confidential
-Go as deep as you can. Do it for yourself not for me or anyone else here.
-There is no wrong to anyone's experience. The 5 energetic principles are a framework for leading you out of the despair of

addiction into permanent sobriety.

-I will refer to CORE Energetics a lot. It is a body work that transforms fixed patterns of behavior. Taps into blocked sources of energy that can keep us stuck in our addictive pattern. It challenges our defenses, belief systems, coping mechanisms, and emotional responses to transform destructive energy into constructive living from our CORE values of love, joy, and happiness.

-You have pens and paper to take notes

-At the end of the weekend each of you will get the course notes that has all the information covered so you can read it.

-I'm not giving it out ahead of time because I don't want to rush the process.

-I am not a psychotherapist. I am not on any medications. I am a healer who is also an interfaith minister.

-There will be mention of spiritual principles

-Everyone's spiritual beliefs are welcomed

-There is no right or wrong way to finding out what that means for you

-After you all get a chance to check in I will share a very personal story that will also introduce you to the 6 Energetic Principles Model

-It is my hope that my vulnerability, tears, whatever comes up will allow you to have the same

-The Intensive is organized as brief teachings, experientials, bodywork, energy movement, and exercises designed to teach you how to overcome addiction. I also give out symbols for you to take with you as reminders. I think this is powerful stuff that solidifies the learning.

-You will leave here after 4 days feeling different. It is my hope that each of you is empowered to live addiction free with this new model of recovery.

-There is nothing wrong with 12-Step recovery or inpatient treatment. This model is just more intense, more confronting, and more body focused.

-I will talk more in the beginning and as the days progress you all will do more talking, feeling, and hard work

-We will have fun too as the agenda suggests.

-Quiet time is just that. A chance for you to integrate in your mind what you need to. Do not make phone calls or watch tv. You can bond with each other.

-Lunch I will eat with you and then leave to prepare. Give you all a chance to talk and reflect without me around.

-No acting out in your rooms. Please no sex, no cigarettes, no substances. For those of you with food issues, let's stick to your food plan. The rooms are blocked from you using television or buying pornography. Please don't masturbate for the 4 days so you can really be present to the feelings.

-The work is intense and beautiful. It is your right to opt out. But be respectful of those that want to participate. If I'm pushing you too hard—please be open to working with that energy. I want the best for all of you.

-If you need help along the way. Raise your hand. Use each other. A special journey and bond will form among all of us. This is sacred work that we are going to do.

-ANY questions

-PARTICIPANT INTRODUCTIONS

FLIP CHART
-Name
-What does addiction mean to you?
-Expectations for the intensive?
-Why you are here?

JEFFREY COHEN PERSONAL STORY AND OVERCOMING ADDICTION

When the crystal meth hustler left my apartment in 2005 I was hanging out the window smoking a cigarette. I just paid him $1,000 cash to give him pleasure and for the ensuing high. The entire world at that moment was a haze of empty hell! As I stared at the courtyard below I reflected on killing myself. My spirit was bankrupt, I couldn't stop smoking cigarettes, drinking alcohol, using meth, and having every form of anonymous sex imaginable.

My gay self- hatred and internalized homophobia repulsed me. Underscoring all these addictions was the escape from an even more insidious addiction—loving unavailable men. Wanting validation and connection with straight friends or guys I never really knew. The substance addictions were just my attempt to not feel the intense pain of being a love addict. Love addiction made me contemplate jumping out that window in 2005. Love addiction cost me my life in ambition, relationships, and my joy, connection to god, and my own happiness was usurped by the preoccupation of a guy that couldn't give a shit about me! I allowed my own energetic system to be hijacked to the point that not having that person's validation lead me to contemplate jumping to my death from my apartment window where I would have been splattered in a courtyard below which was littered with the cigarette butts that I had tossed out the window over the years.

I was desperately bankrupt spiritually. I hated myself and my life. I couldn't go on!

At that same moment, my big, fat, black, cat named Elvira, Louise, Scraps, Sylvia, Cohen who never made a leap in her life came running toward the glass top table near me, with no front claws, she flawlessly jumped onto the glass top table with perfect precision and meowed loudly what sounded like "GET HELP"! I listened. I made arrangements to get into treatment for a life- time of addiction.

I spent $40,000 on in patient treatment. I dialogued, I learned, I hit, I wrote, I processed, I cried, I was the perfect student. I even arranged to meet my CORE therapist every day upon my return after 30 days. As soon as I got off the plane and met up with Elvira Louise in my apartment again—the cat's love wasn't enough to stop another 8- year descent into pure hell.

There are too many facts and too many sordid details to tell you. Suffice to say, that even learning I was HIV + in 2012 did not stop me! All my spiritual training and prayer and meditation did not stop me. Being a Certified CORE Energetics Practitioner and an

Ordained Interfaith Minister didn't stop me.

What stopped me was these 5 energetic principles, a model that draws on all of my experience, but at its genesis is CORE Energetics. I didn't know at the time what I was drawing on. I couldn't even imagine that I remembered learning anything at CORE because for my last two years I was isolated at the hotel after classes, drinking alcohol and smoking cigarettes at night, taking $300 round trip cab rides to unknown towns to have anonymous sex while in the training program. Something called GRACE permeated my recalcitrant addicted self.

It is only after I got sober that I realize I have a model for recovery that can help others. And this model is based on all of my experience, but it is CORE Energetics that made it possible for me to integrate recovery into my life. I now dedicate my work to sharing this model with the gifts that god has provided me: my passion, my connection to spirit, my honest, my ability to explain to complicated people a simple path, my ability to listen, and my love for myself and sincerely wanting to help others.

I now invite you to journey with me on an experience through 5 energetic principles that I'm going to teach you that I used to recover from addiction.

1. ENERGY OF DENIAL Get grounded in reality. I had to stand in front of the mirror and hate what I saw enough to confront my mask that said "fuck-it, I can stop at any time. Or, he's so cute, or just one more. For the addict it is never one more. The last one is never enough! It could never be enough because that is the addict condition.

I had to be punched full of the pain to look at myself. To see a disinterested
passenger in my own life that had boarded the titanic, the sinking ship of addiction, progressive and fatal, and there was only one life-saver! Me.

I will teach you how to get grounded in your body and confront your mask that keeps you in addiction.

-You must get to the place where in your gut it is set that "YOU ARE AN ADDICT" and your mask will kill you! If not a physical death a spiritual death will ensue.

- I am your Elvira Louise Scraps Sylvia Cohen. I'm the cat help you. To stress to you an urgency take you must take this so seriously that nothing else can come above your sobriety!

-I am Jeffrey Cohen and I'm a love addict.

2. ENERGY OF WITHDRWAL Go Through Extended Period of Withdrawal

It does not matter how many therapy sessions, how many prayers, how many magic Lexapro or Prozac pills you take—if the experts don't tell you with all the earnestness at their command that sobriety depends upon a prolonged period of withdrawal they do you a disservice.

I wish someone had been as clear with me as I am about to be with you:

You must withdraw, cease, all addictive behavior, everything all at once, for a period of no less than 6 months. You are not different than me. I thought 30 days and I had it licked. No! 6 months of total and complete withdrawal. No half measures. No but's. You can't stop seeing the hooker but keep your stash of porn. You can't smoke cigarettes and count days off of Alcohol! The kind of sobriety I want for you is the fairy tale. The deep spiritual transformation will only come for you in total and complete withdrawal from all substances, especially if you are cross addicted.

CORE Energetics helped me to feel un- tethered from the addiction. Take this string and hold it tight. This string represents the pull of the addiction. The addict must in understanding Energetic Principle # 2 know that "I can survive withdrawal, separated from the addiction".

Once I felt that separation I had to "go down there" as Gary Rosenthal writes in his poem "The Museum of the Lord of Shame" "south of my predictable borders" "where my soul lay encrusted in the tears I've yet to shed".

But, "you really don't want to go down there", and this is the pull of that addiction, it creates the urgency to turn away. "Many times we turn back from the necessary journey" because we are afraid to meet ourselves!

I had to meet myself in withdrawal, untethered from the addiction. I will lead you today on a journey of meeting yourself. If it scares you—then you are in the right place. If it terrifies you I will teach you to "walk into the void of withdrawal" to meet yourself!

What kept me all those years from meeting myself. It was the emotional incest from my mother that told me at some deep unconscious place that I didn't matter. She took over my energetic system for her needs. So, I never stayed through the withdrawal process. Here's an example of where my internalized rage needed to arrive to take back my energetic system.

This is an example of my writing. I didn't actually do this!

I punch my mother's head through her 72-inch television
Her fear laced blood squirts all over the Natuzzi couches
I spit on the matching pillows and piss on the thousand dollar statues
To her demands for my perfection and emotional soul
I say "NO"!
Even louder I scream "Mine"!

I take the turkey sandwich she just made for me
I make sure I eat every fucking bite of it, because I'll need the strength to take control of my own life! Claim these feelings without one ounce of defense for her. Without one but!

I will help you find the place within you where you matter. Where you feel you can survive the withdrawal!

3. AVOID TOXIC OUTSIDE ENERGY Avoid Toxic People, Places, and Things

I had to avoid all toxic people, places, and things, including ancillary behaviors that triggered the addiction. I had to enforce boundaries with people I liked very much in order not to engage my love addiction. As soon as I felt my energetic system being overtaken, I needed to take it back, often by clearly telling the love object that they are "distracting my recovery". I did this from a place of love, from my higher-self.

The mask presents in CORE Energetics with statements like: "Oh, but we go to the same meetings". "I need that meeting". "Why should they get to go to that meeting and not me".

The energetic idea that you will be confronted with is in its simplest terms: Your survival over their feelings. Or, more broadly stated: You can survive without them or it! .

Here is an example of how I did it. Let's take beautiful CMA Harry who I liked and we were friends. But, I knew he would lead me back to the addiction. You have to understand this is not a forever thing, it is only during the 6 months of withdrawal where you build your self- esteem and identity so no one can over take you.

Let's imagine beautiful Harry standing across from me.
-See Him
"I see you Harry. We are friends. I love to talk to you. But, I must turn my back on you to save my own life!"

Turn your back and feel what happens in your body.

I turn away from him to find my yes to my life at the exclusion of him and all others. With my back turned, I stay with the feelings and transform the excruciating pain of having to set the boundary and losing this friend into "I can survive without you!" This must happen for every addict who is confronted by distraction. I had to be in control of my energetic system to go on my journey!

The toxicity of the constant distraction will prevent the withdrawal and feelings energetic processes from transforming the addict to sobriety. Worse of all, it will cause the addict to relapse!

I will teach you how to find your "yes" energy that allows you to set boundaries for your own recovery. "Hello, Goodbye, and "No" works just fine"!

4. FEELINGS ENERGY: Feel the totality of our feelings and emotions

I had to learn to tolerate my feelings. I had to build a container to house my emotions. This is where I depart from the 12-steps where they ask for removal of what they call defects. A feeling to me is not a defect. It is part of the human condition. We cannot have them removed. It was critical to integrate my feelings—all of them both good and bad!

Fearing my feelings kept me stuck in a purgatory that was annihilating as I ran to one sordid encounter after another to deaden myself from the pain of self- hatred for being gay and its ensuing struggles. I lived a reclusive life, mistaking isolation as being emancipated, free. Free from the demands of people. By not being accountable I lived the belief that people were a burden. The burden would suck me dry. My needs would never be met. So I resigned myself to this life until one day I realized that my seclusion from the world was a prison for my soul. A death of the worst kind!

Mired in sex, love, meth, nicotine, and alcohol addiction for my entire life, it was the spiritual awakening during the withdrawal process that taught me I must feel myself, find god, and emerge to find a place from where I wanted to live.

I used CORE Energetics to consciously get into my body and learn about my feelings.

You are going to learn that consciousness is about setting the intention to do this work.

It was ugly, beautiful and messy, as I went from anxiety and rage to dancing in my heart. I learned that god is real, and he comes to everyone not just the religious or spiritual. It is my free will to say "yes" to this birthright. CORE Energetics is not about punching pillows. It is about finding my spiritual place and learning to wither the ego, in favor of my universal plan of helping others.

FOR EACH OF YOU THIS JOURNEY WILL BE DIFFERENT. BUT I GUARANTEE YOU THAT YOU WILL COME INTO CONTACT WITH YOUR EXISTENTIAL PURPOSE. THAT WILL CAUSE QUESTIONS, FEELINGS, AND SEARCHING FOR SOME LARGER CONNECTION, OR IT MAY NOT. If you are totally sober it is inevitable as a human being to face this condition and make peace with it—contain it in your body, mind, and spiritual framework as these emotions get integrated.

Here is an entry from my journal as it relates to anxiety:

There was a pulse in my childhood home that I never resonated with. The pulse I grew up with was for perfection and order, for nice things, like my Jordache jeans and chocolate velour Izod sweater. But I was always missing something. The anxiety I always felt in the house was the search for my authentic pulse, a validation for the true me to be celebrated in a delicious banquet of give and take and exploration. There was none of that.

The anxiety that I acted out with anonymous sex and crystal meth was the conversation of adoring depth that was always missing. I looked in the mirrors, in the drawers. I put on my mother's shoes and her gorgeous jewelry that rapped around my neck a dozen times. But, it was never to be found. It was elusive--that shared experience of life at depth of nuance, subtlety, original exploration of a journey, a purpose…not just a cliché that the Oprah/Donahue sheep told you to feign. No, not that. I detested that.

And my authentic self was enraged! It was screaming all the time. "I'm a sensitive faggot, boy who wants to feel. See me as original and adore this thinking, feeling, beautiful boy!" And I would retreat like a dog kicked for licking his balls at the family dinner party. And just like the dog I wondered what did I do wrong. Is licking my balls at the dinner table wrong?

Now as an adult I am alone. I sit in early sobriety searching for this pulse. I'm not sure I'll ever find it and it terrifies me. My greatest fear is that I will never be validated for my authentic self.

THE HUMAN CONDITION HAS A MYRIAD OF EMOTIONS THAT MUST BE ACCEPTED, PROCESSED, AND FELT. I never would have found this anxiety if I didn't go through extended withdrawal. I would have just continued acting it out instead of giving it a place now within me that doesn't frighten me to self- destruction.

I will teach you to express, accept, contain, and integrate your feelings!

I check in with myself with intention and consciousness.

The work is never done. I am vigilant. But one thing that is firm: I don't pick up the addiction to escape these feelings.

I'm no saint by any means. But, I have dignity of self.

I learned to build my container and feel my feelings.

You will learn like I did that "I can feel my feelings".

I will teach you to build a container to house your feelings.

The Origins Of Addiction Are Historical usually from early childhood wounding; shame is a family disease.

WHY I AM AN ADDICT?

I have a disease of addiction that originated with my mother and father. We addicts learned not to feel our feelings and there was intense shame on many levels. I had shame, not just for being gay, but for a multitude of things that I inherited from my parents. Shame of my higher self, my love, my joy, my creativity, made me feel wrong for pursuing what I loved. It turns out that my parents passed that onto me because that's how their parents taught them.

SHAME

The model would be grossly incomplete if it did not consider shame and the origins of that shame as family linked. Critical in my healing is the understanding of how I became an addict. It was crucial in accepting feelings of intense shame that I discovered in working the 4th Energetic Principle.

EXISTENTIAL PURPOSE

Transforming shame was critical to exploring my existential purpose, spiritual feelings, and my larger life mission. Shame told me I was wrong. Shame told me god does not exist for me. If I were not able to accept the feelings of shame I never would have allowed god's will for me to be revealed. I also never would have discovered in deep meditation the origins of my love addiction. I would not have felt worthy to dialogue with god to find out the answers.

ORIGINS OF LOVE ADDICTION:

It turns out that my parents had a small part to play in the origins of my love addiction. Love addiction for me originates from the original separation from god. When I incarnated I believed that god left me. That first feeling when I occupied my human body was this insanely frightening and painful thought that I had separated from god—from my source. That never really happened. This is the illusion of the human condition.

The disease of love addiction is a sophisticated defense mechanism that I created to obsess on love objects so that I don't have to feel that initial pain. When I knew in my heart that god never left me, that I only thought he did there was no need to keep creating the illusion. I was free to feel what it is like to be made in god's image, where there are no degrees of worthiness, where god's love for me is the same as you and everyone else.

This spiritual lesson is a journey that was made possible by transforming the shame. This is why it is incumbent upon me to help you:

Understand the origins of your addiction

Understand that addiction is a disease based on shame

Help you accept the feelings of shame so that a transformation happens for you to have the journey to your own spiritual core

5. NEW LIFE ENERGY Slowly Find Healthy Replacements For Addictive Behavior

As addicts we want the answers now! Sitting in uncertainty, vagueness, relationship and sexual abstinence, and even learning our core values must be done slowly. Why? We cannot rush this evolutionary process for so many reasons. But, most important is that it will interfere with building our container to house feelings and may introduce stressors on our withdrawal period.

Slowly find healthy replacements for the addiction. It is paramount for you to do what makes you feel good, joyous, and happy. This is the goal of giving up the addiction. Break isolation and find people with shared interests, find something that nourishes the spiritual part of yourself, read books that you like and do healthy activities that build self esteem. Finding new vocations is a job onto itself. Ask for help and know it is possible.

If this is done slowly with intention and kindness, then it will be for real. You will find a life that is different than you ever imagined. For many they find meaningful love, work, and their spiritual purpose. This can take many months or years of trial and error. Just don't pick up the substance or addiction while building a life worth living.

I will teach you how to consider being aligned to your core values. For me, helping others, being authentic, and having a deep spiritual relationship ranked high. I walked through fear beyond my wildest dreams—over a very extended period of time to arrive here today to speak to you.

I made a plan for a life worth living that you will do as well. This plan changed over time, but one thing that remained at the top of the list is sobriety. Honesty is critical. I did not break free of isolation. I did not make tons of friends and join every group under the sun. As I watched other recovering addicts do this I questioned my path. I compared and despaired! But, as I accepted who I was and my uniqueness it soon be alright to have few friends, go to movies alone, read, have contact with sponsees, and find connection at Career Support Groups and through the help I was able to ask for in counselors and therapists.

Eating well, exercising, and taking good self care are paramount in this discovery phase. I've seen countless addicts jump ship from the titanic into another mayhem of life changing activity just not to feel the vagueness and ambiguity of what is supposed to come next.

This last energetic principle is for each of us to find joy, spiritual fulfillment, and to slowly build a life worth living that brings dignity of self. For me, I still haven't considered fully intimate relationships and my sexual integration. All of this takes time as I'm a work in progress.

CORE Energetics helped me integrate "I can be free", "I can ask for help", "I can fail", "I can be wrong" that allowed me to overcome that rushed feeling of getting everything in its place because time is running out!

I do things I enjoy doing. THIS IS A LIFE WORTH LIVING!

I make sure to keep sobriety first.

I pursue activities, people, and vocations that support my core values.

FACING THE TRUTH PATTERNS OF ADDICTION

TITANIC METAPHOR – SINKING SHIP OF ADDICTION
PATTERN OF ADDICTION WORKSHEET

EACH OF US HAS AN ADDICTIVE PATTERN. THE ADDICTIVE PROCESS STARTS BEFORE WE ACTUALLY BOARD THE TITANIC OF ADDICTION. IDENTIFYING AND CONFRONTING OUR PATTERN IS CRITICAL IN HELPING TO OVERCOME ADDICTION AND AVERTING A SINKING SHIP.

1. EXPLORATION OF PRIMARY ADDICTION_____

2. WHAT SECONDARY ADDICTIONS ARE PRESENT_____,_____
_____,_____
_____.

3. CHOOSE THE MOST RECENT ADDICTIVE EPISODE. EXAMPLE I GOT DRUNK OFF MY FACE AND BLACKED OUT FRIDAY NIGHT

_____
_____
_____

4. WERE YOU AWARE OF SOME UNMET NEED THAT HAPPENED FIRST? EXAMPLE I WANTED SOME VALIDATION FOR DOING A GOOD JOB

_____
_____
_____

5. WERE YOU AWARE OF SOME UNCOMFORTABLE FEELINGS THAT HAPPENED FIRST? EXAMPLE I FELT SHAME THAT I WASN'T AS SMART AS JOHN

_____
_____
_____

6. WHAT IS YOUR MASK STATEMENT BEFORE BOARDING YOUR ADDICTIVE PATTERN? EXAMPLE FUCK IT, IT WON'T BE THAT BAD, I'LL JUST HAVE ONE DRINK, ONE DONUT ISN'T SO BAD……..

The mask statement will have very little energy behind it. It is a statement that we regard as innocuous but we need to confront this as a recognizable pattern. If you cannot recall a specific mask statement recently, pick one that resonates with you: "I'm not addicted, I can stop any time". "I like to have fun and drink with the guys". "I have sexual needs". "Everyone watches porn". "I don't inhale".

_____
_____

ALL ABOARD!
_____
_____

IS IT VERY DIFFICULT FOR YOU TO REVERSE COURSE ONCE AN ADDICT HAS BOARDED THE SINKING SHIP?

IS IT USEFUL TO REMEMBER TITANIC MNEUMONIC AS A REMINDER THAT YOU ARE ACTIVELY ENGAGED IN SOME PHASE OF THE ADDICTION?

TRIGGER
EXAMPLES: MY MOTHER CALLED. MY BOSS DIDN'T LIKE MY WORK.

Identify a Trigger or multiple Triggers:

IMPULSE
EXAMPLES: SAW A GUY SMOKING A CIGARETTE JUST HAD TO HAVE IT, PASSED A RESTAURANT WITH PEOPLE DRINKING BEER AND WENT TO GROCERY STORE……

Provide an example of your impulse behavior

TRAVEL
EXAMPLES: GOING FROM THE COMPUTER TO THE BATHROOM TO MASTURBATE, TAKING A CAB TO THE BAR, WALKING IN A NEIGHBORHOOD WITH DRUG DEALERS

What kind of travel is involved? Think about any movement between rooms, places, etc.

ACTING OUT BEHAVIORS
EXAMPLES: ANONYMOUS SEX, CALLING EX-LOVERS, STALKING, EATING PINTS OF ICE CREAM, SMOKING CIGARETTES, DRINKING LONG AFTER LAST CALL, ETC.

Name Your Specific Acting Out Behavior. If you are cross- addicted name multiple behaviors.

NIRVANA
EXAMPLES: ORGASM, BUZZED, NICOTINE HIT, SUGAR HIGH, "THEY LOVE ME"

Do you drink to get drunk or black out? Do you eat for the high? Do you sex for the orgasm and then you're done?

ISOLATION
EXAMPLES: SEPARATE, ALONE, AVOIDING EVENTS, FEELING DISTANT

What happens after an addictive episode? Do you isolate and want to be alone?

CASTRATION
EXAMPLES: I MADE THE SAME MISTAKE AGAIN, I'M SUCH A LOSER, I FEEL SO B AD ABOUT MYSELF

Do you have feelings of remorse, shame, and guilt at the end of an addictive episode? Do you beat yourself up?

-20 minutes COMPLETE THE PATTERNS OF ADDICTION WORKSHEET
-20 minutes BREAK INTO GROUPS OF TWO PEOPLE AND SHARE
   -LARGER GROUP DISCUSSION
      -What stood out from the exercise?
      -Did you learn anything?
      -Did anything confuse you?
      -Give out the first symbol of the day (life savers)
-50 minutes MASK STATEMENT
      -What is your mask statement. Let's pick one.
      -Challenge the mask
      -Denial to admission
          Volunteer to stand on chair
          Step out into the circle
          Transform I will not surrender

WITHDRAWAL EXPERIENTIAL

-Experience of withdrawal
-You must go through withdrawal for a 6 month minimum
-We will talk about it after the entire experience
-Just note your feelings. Use your pad and paper to write down things to talk about later if you wish.
-Each of you will have to go through this alone. No one can do this for you. It is a singular, precious, gift and the hardest thing you will ever do.
-Each of you has their own station. With your own props.

-String = addiction, -You=addict, Tension = withdrawal
Must understand the varying degrees of pull and tension
Where do you feel it in your body?
What voice does it make to you?
What does it say to you?

CUT THE STRING
STAND SEPARATE FROM THE ADDICTION
YOU ARE NOW SEPARATE AND FREE FROM THE ADDICTION

WALK THE CIRCLE OF UNCERTAINTY
IT IS QUIET AND YOU ARE ALONE

MIRROR :YOU will meet yourself during withdrawal.
Do you like yourself?
Would your childhood self be proud of you or embarrassed of what he/she sees now?

Go into the void of the black paper. Stand in the void of nothingness.
-Read the Gary Rosenthal poem
-lay down on your mats. Play the funeral music.

YOU WILL NEED TO DIE IN ORDER TO LIVE!

FIND THE INNER CHILD THAT YOU ABANDONED. BRING HIM/HER TO YOUR HEART. HOLD THEM CLOSE. YOU WILL NEED TO RECLAIM THEM. PLAY SOME JOYOUS MUSIC...STARTS OFF SLOW AND BUILDS INTO FUN.
-PLAY WITH YOUR GAMES WITH THE INNER CHILD.
-Note to yourself one positive thing about yourself. One thing you like about yourself.

SIT Quietly now.
What are you feeling?

Say to yourself
"I matter"
"I can survive withdrawal"

WITHDRAWAL INTEGRATION

What feelings came up?
Run the energy of withdrawal.
-punch pillows, verbalize,
What happened for you?
Here is the model?
OUR PROCESS GROUP tonight will explore and move the energy that came up in withdrawal.
Transformation of I will not surrender!

PROCESS GROUP NIGHT 1

Music and getting everyone into their bodies
CORE Energetic exercises
Follow the leader
Gentle stretching
Gentle moving

Process group is specifically to work on an issue that came up during withdrawal today. A feeling, thought, belief, something that you need help with from the group. You want to process it further.

SATURDAY AUGUST 24

YOGA NIDRE

Lay on mats
Enjoy guided meditation to relax

AVOIDING TOXIC PEOPLE, PLACES, AND THINGS

3 flip charts, toxic people, places, and things

Each person gets marker

PEOPLE:

GROUP ROLE PLAY-TURN YOUR BACK

PLACE VERBAL BOUNDARY

"MY SURVIVAL MATTERS MORE THAN YOU"

PLACE PHYSICAL BOUNDARY

PLACES:

WHAT IS YOUR PLAN?

RECOIL LIKE A SNAKE?

YES TO MY LIFE

THINGS:

FUCK YOU, SHIT ON YOU, NO –ENERGIZE TO TOXIC THINGS OR SUBSTANCES. FIND **"I CAN SURVIVE WITHOUT YOU"**

FACING FEELINGS

TEACH THE SUMMARY

INTO THE BODY
VERBALIZE, EXPRESS, EXPLORE, TOLERATE
SHAME
RAGE
WITHDRAWAL
CONSCIOUSNESS AND INTENTION
BUILDING A CONTAINER

ROLLER, BREATH, HOLDING
GROUP HELPING EACH OTHER
SUPPORTED

75 MINUTES

INTO YOUR BODY WE GO!

CONCIOUSNESS AND INTENTION

CRITICAL TO BUILDING CONTAINER

What feelings are you most aware of?

Which feeling has the strongest pull to the addiction now?

Talk to me about your feelings.

Shame Messages

Are there any messages of shame from your childhood?

-Call to mind your mother of origin or your primary female care- giver

Ask her "where in my body is the origin of my addiction?"

Allow her to answer and guide your hand to those places. Write them down.

Ask her "what do these places reveal about negative shame messages?"

You can get specific if you wish. For example, if you were constantly called stupid, ask her about that message in particular.

Ask her "how did my shame come about?"

Ask her "Am I holding onto this shame for you as well?"

Now, thank your mother of origin for her help. Before you let go of her image from mind's eye touch one place in your body where shame resides. Rub that place with a firm intention to move that energy free.

Internalized Rage?

Is there any rage you hold onto? How does that feel?

MOVE THE ENERGY

Withdrawal Energy?

Have you been tolerating the withdrawal energy?

ARE YOU AWARE OF ANY POSITIVE FEELINGS? CONNECTION TO SPIRIT, GOD?, LIFE PURPOSE?

-BACK ON ROLLER – BREATH, EXPANSION

-WATERFALL, WIDE OPEN, DEEP BREATH

YOU CAN HOLD THE ENERGY!

-INTEGRATE THE FEELINGS IN THE BODY. I CAN HOLD THESE FEELINGS IN MY CONTAINER.

-I STAY SOBER AND HAVE MY FEELINGS.

PROCESS GROUP FACING FEELINGS

INTO THE BODY
VERBALIZE, EXPRESS, EXPLORE, TOLERATE
SHAME
RAGE
WITHDRAWAL
CONSCIOUSNESS AND INTENTION
BUILDING A CONTAINER

ROLLER, BREATH, HOLDING
GROUP HELPING EACH OTHER
SUPPORTED
Music

GROUP STORY TELLING

Jokes
Talent
Basket of funny questions
  -Most embarrassing moment in your life?
  -TV show you never admit to watching
  -Hidden talent that no one knows about
  -Nicest thing you ever did that you didn't tell anyone
  -Hardest challenge you had to overcome
Play card game

SUNDAY AUGUST 25

FEEL GOOD YOGA

> Gentle Heart Music – walk them through
> Have everyone take turns leading us through what feels good

HEALTHY REPLACEMENTS FOR THE ADDICTION

30 MINUTES

ARE THERE ANY QUESTIONS FROM THE OTHER WORK WE DID?

HOW ARE YOU FEELING WITH THE PROCESS?

CAN YOU SEE HOW THIS WILL HELP YOU STAY SOBER?

30 MINUTES

TELL ME ABOUT A LIFE WORTH LIVING FOR YOU.

-SEX, RELATIONSHIPS, CAREER, SPIRITUAL, SERVICE

WHAT ARE YOUR CORE VALUES?

30 MINUTES

SOBRIETY WILL GIVE YOU A GREAT LIFE.

GO OVER THE TEACHING.

FOCUS ON RUSHED FEELINGS

30 MINUTES

SLOW DOWN THAT RUSHED FEELING

SPEND TIME WITH WITHDRAWAL

BUILD YOUR CONTAINER

LAST SESSION – THINK ABOUT WHAT STILL LURKS?

WHAT DO YOU SEE PREVENTING YOU FROM STAYING SOBER?

NEW LIFE ENERGY PROCESS GROUP

SPRECIIFICALLY WORK ON THAT RUSHED FEELING OR ANGST TO BUILDING YOUR NEW LIFE

THINK ABOUT WHAT STILL LURKS?

WHAT DO YOU SEE PREVENTING YOU FROM STAYING SOBER?

GENERAL PROCESS GROUP

Anything coming up for you?

Feelings of competition?

Anything with me?

Any doubts?

What about withdrawal? Feelings Container?

MOVIE NIGHT

Local cinema.

MONDAY AUGUST 26

SPIRITUAL SERVICE

Spiritual Service – "Heal Thyself"

FINAL PROCESS GROUP

Into their bodies
Mental check and review of what we've done
Review Slide
Experiential
Denial Energy to I am stopped!
Withdrawal Energy – I matter! Success
Toxic Outside Energy – "Me Over You"
Contain Feelings Energy – "I feel and have my sobriety"
New Life Energy – Slowly not rushed "I enjoy"

Anything that lurks?
Scared of leaving?

FAREWELL AND CLOSING REMARKS

All I ask from you is forever to remember me as loving you

Sobriety gives us our hearts, our core, our life's purpose

Each person a chance to talk to the group

Finish Up

SUPPLIES

Name Tags
Flip Chart
Pads
Pens
Survival Bag (Life savers, me, yes, container)
Markers
BLOW UP OF SIX STEP MODEL FOR INTRODUCTION
PRINT OUTS PATTERNS OF ADDICTION WORKSHEETS
Pieces of Rope
Scissors
Mirror
Black Paper – Void
Gary Rosenthal Poem
Funeral Music
Music Player?
Music? Songs? Happy, sad, moving, etc.
Children Games
Fun Music
Set up little stations for each person. Their journey is their own. Withdrawal experiential.
Mats
Pillows
Tennis racquets
cube
Yoga nidre
Heal thyself
Box of tissues
Water
Protein bars, bannanas, fruit.
Decaf coffee
Decaf tea / hot water
Slide of the withdrawal steps in the course notes
HEAL THYSELF

INDIVIDUAL SESSION SCRIPT

SESSION 1: DENIAL ENERGY

Physical Limitations?
Touching during the energy work?
Overview
The work I do is short term, goal driven, to get you sober.
You staying clean from our work together is what matters
I got sober using these 5 principles
I facilitate with you how it is done
You are here so you're open

The model 5 Energetic Principles (15 minutes)
Find out about them (30 minutes)
Pattern of Addiction Worksheet (30 minutes)
Waterfall Grounding (45 minutes)

LET'S WORK ON ENERGY OF DENIAL
Get grounded, "Do you feel here in this moment with me?"
Pick one mask statement from before
Where is that in your body?
Have them hit to move the energy
How was that for you?
What happened to the mask statement in their body?
Confront the denial
   "You will die if you don't stop"
What happened for you?
Can you admit you are an addict?
Feel it in your gut, the transformation of the mask statement to "I will stop now"

For The Next Session
This is your life.
Stay clean until our next session so we can tackle withdrawal energy
Withdrawal is a choice to love your self. Make the choice.
Give client the handouts for denial.

MY NOTES
A.   GET GROUNDED

-Hang over your body and gently massage your toes all the way up to the crown of your head

YOU ARE NOW GROUNDED
From a grounded place (being in the moment) an addict is capable of facing the truth.

B.   FACE THE MASK to FACE THE TRUTH

What is your mask statement?

"I know I have a problem with alcohol, but I can quit at any time"
"Fuck it, it won't feel that bad"
"I haven't lost my job so it can't be that bad"
"I'll just have one more donut and then I'll go on the diet"

C.   FROM DENIAL TO ADMISSION

-Surrender your will. Your will holds on to the mask statement. To overcome addiction we must transform the "I will not give this up" to "I am an addict and it is destroying my life".
-Your addictive pattern is a life long pattern grounded in not wanting to feel uncomfortable feelings.
-Generally some unmet need gets recreated prior to you starting out in your addictive pattern.

Consider your last addictive episode. For example, you got drunk off your face and stayed out all night.

Were you aware of some unmet need prior to embarking on this night of destruction?

Were you aware of some uncomfortable feelings that happened first?

By staying grounded in this admission you will be able to confront the mask. Many intellectuals have written far more than I ever could about the medical processes at work for addicts. Keep it simple.

Addiction is a disease. You are wired for destruction because of uncomfortable feelings. You can change this by admitting to yourself that this exists and getting in touch in your body with the feelings that cause you to run to the addiction.

D.   OTHER GROUNDING METHODS TO FACE THE MASK

-Write it down on paper
-Paint it on a canvas
-Stand on a chair and proclaim it into a room
-Energize the mask by running on a treadmill

The goal of working with denial energy from PRINCIPLE 1 of overcoming addiction is to go from the "no" voice and low energy of denial to the "yes" voice and more energized space within yourself that can surrender to being an addict, that can admit the truth, and have the willingness to transform.
DENIAL ENERGY – "I AM AN ADDICT"

Admission for the addict is the primary step to overcoming addiction. However you get to this place! I personally don't care if you write it on a napkin. You will overcome addiction if you can say "I am addicted" with no reservation. I'm not in favor of a sordid accounting of every horrible thing you did as an addict. I think euphoric recall just serves to add muscle memory and encourage shame that fuels the addictive cycle.

SESSION 2: WITHDRAWAL ENERGY

(rope, black paper hole cut out, poem from Gary Rosenthal)

Check in (are you sober)? (15 minutes)
What happened?
WHAT DO YOU WANT TO DO, PROCEED WITH WITHDRAWAL?
The model 5 Energetic Principles-Withdrawal (15 minutes)
Experiential (light stretching, lead them through core exercises)
a)   Un tethered from addiction (rope, tension, pull, separate)
i. What feelings come up when you are separate?
ii.   Can you survive separation?
b)   Walk to the center of the black hole-the void
i. What comes up in your body
ii.   Can you tolerate the feelings?
iii.   Bring soothing energy to this place
1.   Roller
iv.   Stay in this place of withdrawal

c) Read Gary's Poem
i. You need to meet yourself
ii.   What fears come up about meeting yourself?
d)   Have them claim I Matter
i. What comes up for them when they claim this?
ii.   Reinforce that they matter
iii.   You can do this

Summarize, you are surviving the separation from withdrawal

It is taking you to different places but you are choosing yourself over the pull

6 month extended process—you are going to be challenged! The pull will come

Muscle memory of "I MATTER" – "Withdrawal is a choice to love yourself". The addiction will take you to self hatred.

For The Next Session
This is your life.
Stay clean until our next session so we can tackle withdrawal energy
Withdrawal is a choice to love your self. Make the choice.
Give client the handouts for withdrawal.

MY NOTES

The withdrawal experience from a life time pattern of addiction will bring you to uncomfortable body memories, distorted beliefs in the mind, and a myriad of negative emotions that society claims are bad : examples: anger, internalized rage, jealousy, fear, and pride. An addict in withdrawal will confront these places and must have tools to overcome them and not pick up no matter what. From a Core Energetics perspective most of the time this place is found in the lower self. This is a place that will have a lot of energy, but for many people they don't know how to run that energy or transform it from destroying themselves to a constructive release that will be in service of their higher values and purpose.

The lower self lives in the body and is often part of the armor we carry around. Some like to think about that "stuck feeling" to explain this. Whatever this means for you, you must find a way to dialogue with this place, energize it constructively, and sit with the transformative energy that follows.

A.   STAND UN TETHERED FROM THE ADDICTION

Withdrawal is about staying within you and not giving yourself to the impulse of the addiction. The simplest approach is to feel your separateness from the addiction.

STRING AS THE ADDICTION METAPHOR

-Take a string (symbol the addiction) and attach one end of it to a doorknob. Tie the other end to your belt loop or around your wrist. Exert slight tension. Tension is the symbol of withdrawal. This is what withdrawal feels like when you are tethered to it and going through the process of separation from the addiction. It will pull at you and beckon you to believe that without using you cannot be apart and live.

-Cut the string and notice where in your body you just felt separate from the addiction. Notice if this helped in any way with the feeling of tension. Did this bring you into some uncomfortable feelings?

Whatever exercises you come up with for yourself, the goal here is to understand that through the withdrawal process there will be a tension, a pull to return to the addiction. The lie is that you cannot exist without the addiction. By tethering the addiction, literally cutting it as we did with the string, you teach yourself that you do have the tools to be alone and separate from the addiction.

B. WALK THE UNCERTAINTY EXPERIENCE OF WITHDRAWAL

Once untethered from the addiction an addict will confront the uncertainty and vagueness of who they are and where they are going during the process of withdrawal.

-Use guided meditation to reach this place of uncertainty and do nothing. You will survive. There are free-guided meditations on the Internet.

-Walk a circle in your apartment and consciously hold the place in your body that is uncertain and in withdrawal. Bring awareness to this place as you walk and know that after 5 minutes you have survived. You have taught your mind and body to be separate from the addiction and learn to weather uncertainty that comes up in withdrawal.

C. **FEEL THE DEADNESS IN YOUR BODY DURING THE WITHDRAWAL EXPERIENCE**

Once untethered from the addiction an addict will confront the uncertainty and vagueness of who they are and where they are going during the process of withdrawal.

-Lie down on a hard floor and play funeral music. Stay quiet and have the feeling of death—complete quietness. This will elicit numerous body sensations and feelings. One feeling to notice is where in your body you feel dead without the addiction. This is surely the place that will call to you to pick up. By making friends with this place through dialogue, soothing touch, and acceptance it's power over you will diminish.

D. **RUN THE ENERGY OF NEGATIVE FEELINGS THAT COME UP DURING WITHDRAWAL**

Withdrawal energy may manifest itself as anxiety and rage. Find a way to run this energy from your body. This means releasing it in a constructive way. In CORE Energetics we energize and make sure to discharge it. Please note that the discharge may take you to other feelings. Just stay with the process and don't pick up no matter what.

Some techniques to use:

-Exaggerated Story
Use your voice to match the energy and intensity of the feelings.
Verbalize the feelings in a story.
For example, "I gotta have the nicotine now…..NOW, NOW, give it to me, I want it, I need it….".
Curse, scream, and exaggerate the addictive pull.

-Punching pillows
-Sprints at the gym
-Screaming in your car "Not another fucking day of this!"
-Kicking, Boxing, Deep Knee Bends
-Laying In Bed And Alternating Kicking and Punching

E. **AFER RUNNING THE ENERGY OF WITHDRAWAL, INTEGRATE THE REMAINING EMOTIONS INTO YOUR WILL, BODY, MIND, AND SPIRIT**

After discharging the withdrawal energy you will be left with emotions. These now have to be contained in your body, mind, spirit, and will centers. For each of us this will be very different. Keep it simple. If the tears flow, let them flow. Gary Rosenthal says in "The Museum of the Lord of Shame" that our soul is encrusted in salt from the tears we've yet to shed." Crying is beautiful!

-"Wow, I understand withdrawal is a process and I can survive"
-"My inner child needs a hug and I'm going to give him one"
-"I'm a good person and I just made it through an addictive urge"
-"Picking up is not negotiable, no matter what"
-"I just met a part of myself and that wasn't so terrible"
-"Withdrawal sucks, but this guy Jeffrey Cohen says I can do it!"

You will meet yourself in ways you never imagined. Have the experience for yourself and know how precious it is. This time in your life when you look back on it will be monumental in how it prepared you for a life purpose you never imagined possible in the addiction.

WITHDRAWAL ENERGY PRINCIPLE 2 – "I CAN WITHDRAW", "I MATTER"

Withdrawal must be done perfectly. That means no picking up the addiction under any and all circumstances. I don't entertain notions of relapse because it is not an option. Not negotiable. This is where I diverge with therapists and inpatient treatment. I'm not interested in having you as a client for life. Unfortunately, many of these treatment businesses make their money from chronic-relapsers who don't receive this message as strongly as I'm conveying it to you.

However you do it, with whatever technique you find works for you. I don't care if it is taking long walks with your dog or watching re-runs of the Golden Girls—you must go through an extended withdrawal process that will last at least 6 months. During this time you will have fun, too. It is not all hell and anguish. But, I will tell you that the darkest hours for any addict come during this period. No bullshit.

And the goal of moving through withdrawal is for you to be able to claim:

I CAN WITHDRAW FROM _____ ADDICTION

And from the accomplishment of withdrawal through addiction belies a self-esteem that develops slowly revealing the authentic person you were meant to be. You integrate in your body, mind, will, spirit, and emotional framework a very simple, powerful, guiding life affirming foundation:

I MATTER

SESSION 3: TOXIC OUTSIDE ENERGY

(FLIP CHART PAPER AND MARKERS)
Draw on your notes from the pattern of addiction worksheet

Check in (are you sober)? (15 minutes)
HOW IS WITHDRAWAL?
Deep knee bends, ocular massage, self-body check in

Toxic People, Places, Things you need to avoid for sobriety
Marker and fill in the list (15 minutes)

Pick a toxic person (60 minutes)
How would it feel to set a boundary?
Set a boundary
See the person
Turn Your Back
Verbal boundary
How was that?
Work with "I can never do that"? Why not?
Energize: they matter more than me.
"I can't"

PLACE VERBAL BOUNDARY
"MY SURVIVAL MATTERS MORE THAN YOU"
Energize the "No, I can never do that"

PLACE PHYSICAL BOUNDARY
PLACES:
WHAT IS YOUR PLAN?
RECOIL LIKE A SNAKE?
YES TO MY LIFE

THINGS:
FUCK YOU, SHIT ON YOU, NO –ENERGIZE TO TOXIC

THINGS OR SUBSTANCES. FIND "I CAN SURVIVE WITHOUT YOU"

"Me over you"

Teaching
Wrap Up
Review denial energy, withdrawal energy, toxic outside energy
How are you doing with this work?

TOXIC OUTSIDE ENERGY-MY NOTES
Yes, you do!
From a Core Energetics perspective, boundaries exerted from a higher-self place feel better when originated in the intention of self-love. It is not something bad being done to another person, but an act of kindness to the self. Having said this I have placed boundaries to avoid many people while in recovery from my lower-self place, where I felt the energy of "fuck you I'm going to live even if you die".

I don't recommend setting boundaries from the mask. The mask feels inauthentic and will produce feelings of guilt and shame over time. The mask would make excuses. The higher-self tells the truth about why they need to avoid a person or substance or event. Higher-self energy comes from the heart; detaching with love.

Whatever you call it, remember to "recoil like a snake" when it feels in your body like your sobriety can be jeopardized. You will most probably feel the sensation in your body that a person, event, or being around a thing is not good for your recovery. Honor it. Trust it.

Whatever this means for you, you must find a way to shift your energy to saving yourself above all else. This is the sensation that needs to be integrated into your body, mind, and will in order to maintain sobriety.

A.   Your "Yes" to Life Matters More Than Anything

Feel the sensation of your "yes" to life trumping all others.

Toxic Person Example – Turning Your Back
- The easiest way is to stand in front of a closed door. Imagine that person standing across from you. Acknowledge that person out loud.
o Then, turn your back to that person.
o Say out loud "I'm sorry_____, I matter more than you".
You will feel a shift of energy into your power and resolve.

Continuing on with the above example.

-THE MASK ENERGY would apologize profusely and go into a million explanations

-The LOWER SELF ENERGY would say "Fuck You", "Shit On You", "No"

-The HIGHER SELF-ENERGY would say "I love you but I love myself more"

The above dialogues are to be had alone with yourself. They are used in the service of finding your "yes" that places sobriety above all distractions from that.

B. You will survive without another person, place, or thing. Knowing this in your mind, body, and spirit is crucial to stay firm in your boundary.

Guided Meditation – Save Yourself In The Life Boat

-Imagine you are in a plane crash. There is only one oxygen mask hanging above you and another person. Grab that mask.

-Where did you feel that in your body?

-Remember that place in your body and plant the "yes to your life" there

-Without a shift to saving one self above all else, the addict will relapse

C. Recognition that half measures avail you nothing in setting boundaries is crucial.

If you have difficulty with this I recommend you energize the place within you that says "No, I can't stop going to that place or seeing that person even though I know they will lead to me picking up"

-Punch some pillows and say "No, I can't stop"

-After some time of doing this stand up straight and ground the energy you just created into your body.

-Do the same punching again into the pillow and say "No, I won't stop"

Stand up again

See if this leads you on a journey to understand why you would allow a toxic person to take precedence over you.

TOXIC OUTSIDE ENERGY GOAL – "I CAN SURVIVE WITHOUT YOU"

Avoiding toxic people and places is very difficult for addicts to do. It is much easier to do if you have support from a group. I cannot stress enough that the goal of avoiding people, places, and things is to not trigger your addiction. It is to give you the best chance to stay clean and move through withdrawal. Maybe after a period of 6 months you can go to these places, or be around the toxic person you put down. Only you can decide that in an honest moment.

Making the choice that "I can survive without you" is a critical shift in consciousness. In CORE Energetics this also referred to as bringing awareness and intention to a situation. Do not underestimate toxic people and places. However you need to do it, arrive at a place within yourself where you believe with all your heart that "I can survive without you". This will aid you immensely as you move through withdrawal and it will allow you to focus on recovery. Recovery takes a lot of energy. Don't let distractions divert you from your primary purpose.

SESSION 4: FEELINGS ENERGY

30 minutes
Get them right on the roller
And simultaneously go into the teaching

75 MINUTES
INTO YOUR BODY WE GO!
CONCIOUSNESS AND INTENTION
CRITICAL TO BUILDING CONTAINER

What feelings are you most aware of?
Which feeling has the strongest pull to the addiction now?
Talk to me about your feelings.

Shame Messages
Are there any messages of shame from your childhood?
-Call to mind your mother of origin or your primary female care-giver
Ask her "where in my body is the origin of my addiction?"
Allow her to answer and guide your hand to those places. Write them down.
Ask her "what do these places reveal about negative shame messages?"
You can get specific if you wish. For example, if you were constantly called stupid, ask her about that message in particular.
Ask her "how did my shame come about?"
Ask her "Am I holding onto this shame for you as well?"

Now, thank your mother of origin for her help. Before you let go of her image from mind's eye touch one place in your body where shame resides. Rub that place with a firm intention to move that energy free.

Internalized Rage?
Is there any rage you hold onto? How does that feel?
MOVE THE ENERGY

Withdrawal Energy?
Have you been tolerating the withdrawal energy?

ARE YOU AWARE OF ANY POSITIVE FEELINGS? CONNECTION TO SPIRIT, GOD?, LIFE PURPOSE?

-BACK ON ROLLER – BREATH, EXPANSION
-WATERFALL, WIDE OPEN, DEEP BREATH
YOU CAN HOLD THE ENERGY!

-INTEGRATE THE FEELINGS IN THE BODY. I CAN HOLD THESE FEELINGS IN MY CONTAINER.

-I STAY SOBER AND HAVE MY FEELINGS.

LAST 15 MINUTES
INTEGRATE, TALK, ANYTHING COMING UP FOR YOU AROUND THE WORK?
STAY SOBER AND PRACTICE THIS.

FEELINGS ENERGY: MY NOTES

Some addicts find it useful to feel the competitiveness in their bodies in order to reach the goal of "I can survive without you". This competitive spirit can serve you in taking your will back constructively in the service of your sobriety.

Core Energetics practice allows for human beings to build a container for feelings. In its simplest terms you learn how to tolerate and be with all of your feelings while being stone cold sober from all addictions. Many of the tools for building this container I have used from Alexander Lowen's Bionergetics. I'm not about to write a treatise on the differences between Core Energetics and Bionergetics. I've taken the best of both disciplines and applied it to our model to save our butts (literally!) from killing ourselves with addiction. Don't get bogged down in terminology—get bogged down in the seriousness of recovery and building this human container that only you can hold for yourself.

Building your own human container for tolerating feelings depends on consciousness and intention. Consciousness is mindful awareness and intention required committed, purposeful action. If you bring both of these to the process of building your human container you will be amazed at how your feelings will be housed within your body. It will be a new experience of life for many addicts. We spent our lives running from feelings. Now, we are being asked to house and contain them. Be loving and be gentle through this exploration. But, do it!

It is presented here in order. But feelings are not ordered. Any one of these steps can occur at any time. You could already be in touch with your feelings without having to get grounded. This is just a model. The real world is far more complex.

A.   Into The Body

Most people dread getting grounded in their bodies with the intention to feel feelings.

BODY INVENTORY
-The simplest way into the body is the body inventory. Bend over with bent knees and use your hands to support the ground. Feel the tension in your legs. Focus on your breath and deeply breathe so that your belly feels full and then releases. Then just begin touching from your toes all the way up your body. Include touching all genital areas. Our sexuality is not something to be ashamed of. We are just bringing awareness to all parts of our body.
-After a few minutes of this exploration gently come up into a standing position and flex your chest area out into the world. Continue to focus on your breathing and notice that you have entered your body. Welcome Home!

There are thousands of ways to get into the body:
-deep knee bends
-kicking
-hitting
-exercise
-rollers
-bouncing on exercise balls
-dancing to music
-yoga

-guided meditation

Just pick one that resonates for you and is safe physically but it allows you to open up to your feelings.

B.   Notice What Feelings You Meet When Your In Your Body

How do you feel when you get into your body?

Remember we are bringing conscious awareness to feelings that we unconsciously used our addiction to not feel. Now, we are saying to these feelings I'm going to have a dialogue with you and welcome you into my human container. "Make friends with your feelings". Welcome them. This is a very different approach for us addicts to entertain. We were accustomed to running for the substance at the first sign of a feeling.

C.   Express to yourself some of the more uncomfortable feelings that are present in the moment (either good or bad). For example, pain, guilt, anger, shame, lonely, anxious, fear, happy, tired, hungry

What feelings are present?
Where in your body do you feel your feelings?

D.   Bring your feelings into the light. Physicalize them and express them to the world. Notice how you can move from feelings of anger to love to sadness to joy. Notice the historical links to mother and father or significant defining moments from childhood.

Let's take anger as an example. You are aware of a feeling of being angry at someone. In CORE Energetics we might want to express lower-self energy.

-Punch some pillows and scream out loud "I hate you"
-Punch these pillows even more and scream even louder "I hate you"
-See where these feelings take you
-You might confront a new feeling of "fear" or it may take you into your core feelings of love and joy and happiness. More often than not it will trigger some feeling from long ago, a historical reminder of some childhood feeling that was stored in your body.
-By bringing it into the light and having a dialogue with it we learn to distinguish amongst our feelings and start to understand the origins.

-We don't run from our feelings into the addiction. We find healthy ways to express them and integrate them in our bodies.

D. For some people they come into contact with trauma from childhood. These were events where their emotional framework was violated. Abuse, neglect, rape, etc. Only you know how much you can handle and what level of support you need to process them. If the terror is so overwhelming that it renders you incapacitated—seek a trained therapist for support.

For many other people the physical aspects of moving blocked energy and stimulating their bodies where memories were trapped bring them in contact with long repressed wounding. These feelings for addicts are hard to handle. Just know that feelings don't kill you. Addictions kill you.

Common CORE Energetic Wounds:
- Schizoid Wound – "I don't exist", "Not welcomed in the world", "Existential Crisis", "Separation from spirit", etc.
- Masochistic Wound – "My energy was overtaken and I'm not giving anything to you", "I withhold from you because you took it from me", "No way!", etc.
- Oral Wound - "I can't take care of myself", "I need and I'm afraid my needs won't be met", "I can't stand on my own two feet", etc.
- Rigid Wound – "My sexuality is shameful", "I struggle to feel love and sex at the same time", "Being in my heart is difficult when I make love", "Integrating sex and love is very confusing so I want to run away", etc.
- Psychopathic Wound – "I don't trust", "I will reject you before you reject me", "I will not get into my body because I'm too afraid to feel my grounding to earth because it isn't safe", etc.

If you are interested in CORE Energetics research on your own. My website has links to some good sites. My point for this model is not to teach CORE Energetics per se, but to provide enough information for you to understand a new way to feel feelings toward building the container.

E. We Accept Our Feelings and As We Physicalize Them We Observe The Transformation In Our Bodies, Mind, Will and Spirit

The transformation of feelings into energy that just is takes practice and time.

Deep Breathing
-Stand up tall and open your arms wide. Breathe deeply and fully into

your body. Hold all the feelings in the container of your body.
   -Notice what happens in the body.
   -Notice what your thinking.
   -How about your spiritual place?
   -And, what about your self will that ran to the addiction?
   -What have you learned during this transformative process?

Transformation is magical and it means different things for different people. But, most of the time the transformation allows us to move from negative places within ourselves into living in our heart center. From our heart center we don't want to destroy ourselves. Living in the CORE is the goal of CORE Energetics and is the goal of many recovering addicts.

   E.   We Have Now Built Our Human Container. It houses the exceptional emotional framework of feelings that we as humans experience.

ENERGETIC PRINCIPLE 4 GOAL – "I CAN FEEL MY FEELINGS", "I CONTAIN MY FEELINGS"

The goal is to contain your feelings and integrate them into your life in a positive way. Over time the container you build gets solidified and holds us in check. We start to trust the different places in us and even start living from intuition and spiritual guidance. For purposes of overcoming addiction you will arrive at the following declarations:

- I am ready to face feelings of _____, _____, _____.

- I can feel my feelings and not use my addiction!

- I contain my feelings and integrate them within my body, mind, and spiritual framework.

It is wonderful to learn how complex we are. I guarantee you once you build this container and know it is for real you will be lead on a journey to internal places and dialogue never imagined. Again, don't pick up the addiction! Feel your feelings and constructively express them in new passions over time.

Critical in every addict's healing is the understanding of how they became an addict. It is crucial in accepting feelings of intense shame that are discovered in working the 4th Energetic Principle. CORE Energetics welcomes the truth of our past as a teacher for future freedom to live in our hearts.

Most people list their family members going back several generations and identify addictions and behaviors that were passed on. Included in this list were the negative family messages and the shame based teaching that was the family's lineage. Others ask family members still living to fill in the blanks, or use spirit guides to obtain information about our family of origin. Others will open dialogue with close friends to draw out this information.

You are encouraged to get the answers you seek any way that resonates for you. For purposes of the workshop and course I'm presenting a creative approach because I want participants to take a risk to harness their creative energy in the service of healing. I reiterate there are many roads you can take to understand the family origins of addiction and shame.

CORE Energetics looks to the body for its answers.

Do this exercise for yourself. You only share the answers if you are moved to do so.

Part 1

-What Does Your Body Tell You About The Origins of Addiction and Shame?

-Stand in front of a mirror with gym clothes so you can see as much of your body as possible. Have a pen and paper on a chair near by for easy access.
-Take time reviewing your own body completely.
-Do this yourself without any music or distraction.
-Suspend all judgment now and negative talk about what your body looks like.

-Call to mind your mother of origin or your primary female care-giver
Ask her "where in my body is the origin of my addiction?"
Allow her to answer and guide your hand to those places. Write them down.
Ask her "what do these places reveal about negative shame messages?"
You can get specific if you wish. For example, if you were constantly called stupid, ask her about that message in particular.
Ask her "how did my shame come about?"
Ask her "Am I holding onto this shame for you as well?"

Now, thank your mother of origin for her help. Before you let go of her image from mind's eye touch one place in your body where shame resides. Rub that place with a firm intention to move that energy free.

Tell Her: "I will now use this energy of shame in the service of finding and developing my core values".

Please note that you are telling her not asking her.
Notice in your body without writing anything down what you felt.

-Call to mind your father of origin or your primary male care-giver
Ask him "where in my body is the origin of my addiction?"
Allow him to answer and guide your hand to those places. Write them down.
Ask him "what do these places reveal about negative shame messages?"
You can get specific if you wish. For example, if you were constantly called stupid, ask him about that message in particular.
Ask him "how did my shame come about?"
Ask him "Am I holding onto this shame for you as well?"

Now, thank your father of origin for his help. Before you let go of his image from mind's eye touch one place in your body where shame resides. Rub that place with a firm intention to move that energy free.

Tell Him: "I will now use this energy of shame in the service of finding and developing my core values".

Please note that you are telling him not asking him.
Notice in your body without writing anything down what you felt.

Part 2

-Bringing Intention and Consciousness To Using Shame Energy In The Service of Finding and Developing CORE values

-Sit down for this, but keep your notebook with you. Turn to a new clean page.
-Let the released shame energy from part 1 serve you here. It has been released.
-Let the released shame energy from part 1 answer this question.

"What are your core values?" List at least 1.

Meaning what values do you want in your sober life.

Examples can be courage, love, compassion, service, etc. Make them your own.

Part 3

Heart of Values
-Pick one core value from your list. Example love.
-Imagine that core value.
- -Lay completely flat on the floor
-Take your hands and hold that core value. Really bring intention to holding it, seeing it in your mind's eye.
-Very slowly move your hands holding that core value to your heart.
-Release that value to your heart.
-Lay Still
-After some time repeat this out loud "I am worthy"

Part 4

Existential Purpose and Spiritual Connection
-From your heart let the core value answer this question
What is my life purpose?
-Be with the question and the journey wherever it takes you.
-Lay Silent, Be Still, Be Safe.
What is the universal plan for me?
FEELINGS ENERGY PRINCIPLE 4 GOAL – "I ACCEPT FEELINGS OF SHAME AND THEIR ORIGIN", "I FIND I HAVE CORE VALUES", "I AM WORTHY TO FIND MY UNIVERSAL PLAN AND PURPOSE"

Demonstrated in this principle is that shame can be used in the service of finding your core values and ultimately send you on your exploration to finding your life plan in the larger universe.

This is an experience for you to repeat over and over. This principle attempts to convey concepts that are intensely individual. Do not get frustrated or defeated if you had trouble with this. You will find your own way to accept feelings of shame and know that you are worthy to explore existential questions.

CORE Energetics Recognizes The Human versus the Spiritual

As feelings get exposed the human (material) world versus the spiritual world(our journey and connection to something bigger inside or outside of us) will reveal itself. Each of us must decide as humans how to integrate this in our daily life and what practices we want to pursue. There are manifestos written on these topics—all I'm trying to do is encourage you with this recovery model to not shy away from your own discovery and journey. Later on in my story I will take a risk and share mine. You are encouraged to have your own expression.

Some helpful ideas to take away:
- Understand the origins of your addiction

- Understand that addiction is a disease based on shame

- Accept feelings of shame and their origin so a transformation happens for you to have the journey to your own spiritual core

SESSION 5: NEW LIFE ENERGY

30 MINUTES
ARE THERE ANY QUESTIONS FROM THE OTHER WORK WE DID?
HOW ARE YOU FEELING WITH THE PROCESS?
CAN YOU SEE HOW THIS WILL HELP YOU STAY SOBER?

30 MINUTES
TELL ME ABOUT A LIFE WORTH LIVING FOR YOU.
-SEX, RELATIONSHIPS, CAREER, SPIRITUAL, SERVICE

WHAT ARE YOUR CORE VALUES?

30 MINUTES
SOBRIETY WILL GIVE YOU A GREAT LIFE.
GO OVER THE TEACHING.
FOCUS ON RUSHED FEELINGS

30 MINUTES
SLOW DOWN THAT RUSHED FEELING
SPEND TIME WITH WITHDRAWAL
BUILD YOUR CONTAINER
LAST SESSION – THINK ABOUT WHAT STILL LURKS?

STAY SOBER

MY NOTES - NEW LIFE ENERGY
- In order to maintain sobriety daily connection to healthy behavior is paramount to maintain the dignity of self and blessings that accrue to addicts who have successfully navigated total withdrawal. As part of our feelings container we define our core values that make up our higher self. We get in touch with these values daily through our own spiritual practice or routine. This can be using yoga, prayer, meditation, painting, journals, deep breathing, stretching, or exercise.

PART 1
CORE VALUES DECLARATION
- -I (NAME) claim the following core values as my own.

PART 2
A LIFE WORTH LIVING
- -Using a large drawing pad and markers, please create a picture, poem, writing, song, road map, etc. that conveys "A LIFE WORTH LIVING"
- -include sobriety, professional, personal, sexual, and family relationships
- -include things you enjoy, get specific, like watching "Survivor"
- -include how this is aligned to your core values

PART 3
MAKE IT REAL
- -Share it with the group or with a trusted friend
-

PART 4
ASK FOR HELP
- -Note one item on your life worth living that you need help to realize.
- -Choose a member of the group and ask them for help.

PART 5
HONESTLY ANSWER: WHAT HAPPENS IF I TRY SOMETHING AND FAIL?
- -Share one risk that you contemplate taking and what happens if you fail?
- -"Hear another member reply, but you have a sober life".

PART 6
THE RUSH IS ON
- -Feel into your body and imagine yourself living this new life. What

pressure consumes you, what rushed feeling lurks?
- Name it into the room now.
- To that pressure or rush you must be clear: "Sobriety First! I will get to you."

PART 7
CELEBRATION OF OUR HEARTS
- "ALL I ASK FROM YOU IS FOREVER TO REMEMBER ME AS LOVING YOU"
- MUSICAL INSPIRATION

NEW LIFE ENERGY PRINCIPLE 5 GOAL – "I AM ALIGNED TO MY CORE VALUES", "I DO THINGS I ENJOY", "I CAN ASK FOR HELP", "I CAN FAIL", "SOBRIETY IS A LIFE WORTH LIVING"

- SHARING YOUR HEARTS, CORE VALUES, AND LIFE PLAN WILL SERVE YOU IN FINDING JOY AND FULFILMENT IN YOUR LIFE.

- I do things I enjoy doing.

- I make sure to keep sobriety first.

- I pursue activities, people, and vocations that support my core values.

- This is a life worth living!

- Slowly, so I can build my container that houses my feelings so I can really know what thrills me without the addiction.

SESSION 6: SUMMARY

30 MINUTES
ANY QUESTIONS
ARE YOU SOBER?
TEACHINGS SUMMARY – REVIEW ENERGY GRID

30 MINUTES
YOGA NIDRE

30 MINUTES

SPIRITUAL EXPLORATION
LEVEL OF THE SOUL
MORE ENERGY WORK
REINFORCE THE CONTAINER

30 MINUTES
FEELINGS OF GOOD BYE
SACRED WORK
I'M HERE FOR YOU IF YOU NEED ME

Jeffrey C.

ABOUT THE AUTHOR

Jeffrey Cohen is a recovery expert and spiritual powerhouse. Mr. Cohen is a Certified CORE Energetics Practitioner and Ordained Interfaith Minister. From his time spent in deep journey to god he has channeled this book to revolutionize addiction treatment. From the depths of his own 18 year struggle to overcome addiction he has delivered to addicts a model for living. In his elegant prose he has captured the simplicity of transforming destructive energy to get real and get sober! Mr. Cohen has taken us on an epic triumph to finding how to say "I MATTER" amidst the blocked energy of our wounded souls. What an expression of pure delight that Mr. Cohen has found recovery, and taken the time to share his master piece with the world.

He builds for all of us a container not just to house feelings, but a road map for mastering life. Overcoming addiction is proof that recovery produces miracles. Behold our latest miracle, Jeffrey Cohen.

Here is the real power for addicts:

1. **Unblock Denial Energy**. Urgently confront your denial and blocked energy to get you un-stuck and willing to save your own life

☐ 2. **Separate From Withdrawal Energy**. Stand separate from your addiction to claim "I MATTER", the necessary resolve needed to go through total withdrawal

☐ 3. **Avoid Toxic Outside Energy**. You avoid toxic people, places, and things by transforming "no I can't" body energy to "MY SURVIVAL MATTERS MOST"

☐ 4. **Contain Feelings Energy**. You must contain the experience of all of your feelings (good and bad) so that you don't get overwhelmed into relapse

☐ 5. **Slowly Integrate New Life Energy**. You let recovery sink-in slowly and stay sober! ☐ You learn to handle "rushed energy" that comes up when creating a new sober life.
☐

☐ Any addict can use this model to overcome addiction if they are ready to get real and get sober!

Printed in Great Britain
by Amazon